SPORTS

Written by

EMILIE DUFRESNE

Designed by

DANIELLE RIPPENGILL

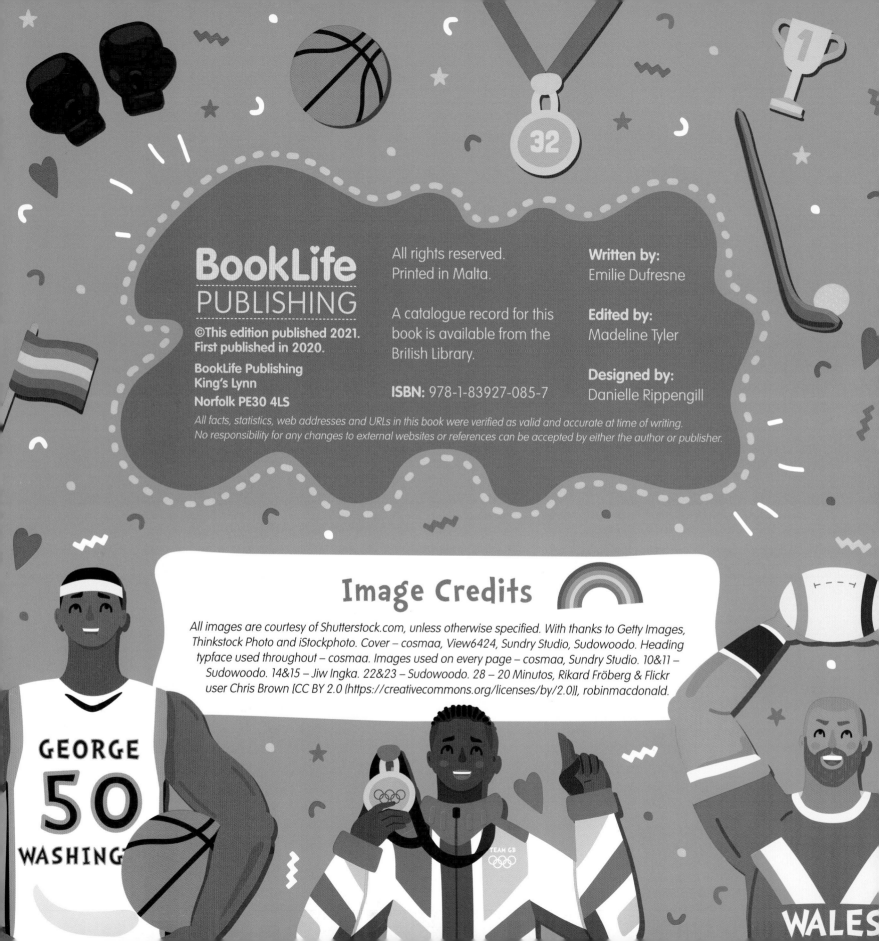

BookLife
PUBLISHING

©This edition published 2021.
First published in 2020.

BookLife Publishing
King's Lynn
Norfolk PE30 4LS

A catalogue record for this
book is available from the
British Library.

ISBN: 978-1-83927-085-7

Written by:
Emilie Dufresne

Edited by:
Madeline Tyler

Designed by:
Danielle Rippengill

Image Credits

CONTENTS

Words that look like this are explained in the glossary on page 30.

HAVING PRIDE

What Does It Mean to Have Pride?

Pride is a feeling or emotion that someone can have. A person might feel proud of something they have achieved or feel proud of who they are. It is also possible to feel proud of other people, who they are, and what they have achieved.

What Is Pride?

As well as being a feeling or emotion, Pride is the name given to an event that happens in many places around the world. The event often includes a march and celebration for the LGBTQIA+ community. Pride is a time for people in the LGBTQIA+ community to celebrate and have pride in who they are. It is also a time for people to talk about what still needs to be done for the LGBTQIA+ community.

LOVE IS LOVE

What Does LGBTQIA+ Mean?

LGBTQIA+ is an abbreviation of letters that mean different things about a person's sex, sexuality and gender identity.

Sex

A person's sex is to do with their biology. It can refer to the biological sex they were assigned at birth, or it could be the sex they identify with.

Sexuality

Sexuality is a way of talking about a person's sexual identity. This is to do with the ways in which a person may or may not feel attracted to people, and what people they are attracted to.

Gender Identity

Gender identity is a person's idea of how they are masculine, feminine, a mixture of these, or neither of them.

5

A Closer Look at the Letters

There are lots of different versions of the LGBTQIA+ abbreviation that people might use to describe the community. Each letter means a different thing. As we learn more and more about sex, sexuality and gender identity, more letters and meanings are included in the abbreviation.

Bisexual
This is a person who is attracted to more than one gender.

Transgender
This is when a person's gender identity is different to the biological sex they were assigned at birth.

Gay
This can be men or women who are only attracted to people who are the same sex as them.

Lesbian
This is a woman who is only attracted to other women.

Many people think of the rainbow flag as a sign for the LGBTQIA+ community. The flag shows that even though people are different, it is these differences that are beautiful. It is time to celebrate and share pride in the achievements of sportspeople who are members of the LGBTQIA+ community.

Queer

Someone might see themselves as queer if they feel their sexual and gender identities are anything other than heterosexual or cisgender.

Intersex

This is a person who is born with a mixture of sex characteristics that are seen as male and female, such as genitals and chromosomes.

Asexual

This is a person who does not feel sexually attracted to any sex or gender.

Plus

This is used to include all the letters that are missing from the abbreviation and to make sure everyone in the LGBTQIA+ community feels included regardless of who they are. This can include people who are pansexual or gender fluid.

GARETH THOMAS

Born: 1974

> There may be an 18-year-old who put his rugby boots away because he was gay and thought he wouldn't be accepted, but now he can go back to the cupboard and dust his boots down.

A Rising Talent

Gareth Thomas was a very successful Welsh rugby player. He started playing in a youth club in Bridgend, UK, and went on to play for other clubs in Europe. He then went on to represent Wales for over ten years. After battling with injury, he retired from rugby in 2011.

Let's Talk About Sexuality

In 2009, Gareth publicly announced that he was gay. This made him the first openly gay rugby union player. Gareth hoped that by being open about his sexuality he would encourage other people in sports to be more open about sexuality.

WALES

Achievements

- First Welshman to win 100 <u>caps</u> in rugby union
- Captained Wales' Grand Slam winning team in 2005
- Awarded BBC Wales Sports Personality of the Year in 2005

Sportspeople and Sexuality

Many sportspeople choose not to tell the public about their sexuality or gender identity if it is anything other than heterosexual and cisgender. This is because sports events are often split into different categories such as men's and women's, so many people worry that they would be treated differently if they were open about who they are. There are also lots of gender <u>stereotypes</u> in many sports that make people feel uncomfortable about telling people about their sex, sexuality and gender identity.

FALLON FOX

Born: 1975

A Hit Above

Fallon Fox is a **professional** MMA fighter. This stands for mixed martial arts. She began wrestling in high school and went on to join the **military** for four years. After transitioning from male to female, Fox started training in MMA and went on to become professional.

Putting the 'I' in Identity

Fallon was assigned male at birth. From a very young age she remembers questioning her gender identity. Growing up as a teenage male, Fallon thought she was a gay man until she learnt about what it means to be transgender. Later on, she went on to transition to female. By publicly announcing that she was transgender, she has become a role model for transgender people in sports.

What Is Transitioning?

A transgender person may or may not choose to transition. Transitioning means a different thing to every person. It might involve medical transitioning, such as taking medication or having surgery. For someone else, it could involve telling friends and family, dressing differently and changing their name to one they feel suits them more.

It's not about the genitals they have between their legs, it's not the chromosomes they can't see. It's the thing located inside their <u>cranium</u>.

Achievements

- First openly transgender female MMA fighter
- Became a member of the National Gay and Lesbian Sports Hall of Fame in 2014
- Won five out of six fights as a professional MMA fighter

HELEN AND KATE RICHARDSON-WALSH

Helen Born: 1981 - Kate Born: 1980

> We're so lucky to be hockey players. Everyone is just accepted for who they are.

Going for Gold

Kate and Helen Richardson-Walsh both played hockey together and were both on the Great British team for many years. They became a couple in 2008 and married in 2013. They have played in four Olympic tournaments together. The fourth of these was the 2016 Olympic Games and it was here that the Great British team went on to win a gold medal. This made them the first married gay couple to win an Olympic gold medal together.

HELEN

Family Matters

Since their retirements, Helen and Kate have started a family. They are now <u>activists</u> who give talks to students to <u>normalise</u> LGBTQIA+ relationships. They have also raised <u>awareness</u> for LGBTQIA+ players in sport and they hope that by being open about their relationship, it will make other sports as accepting of the LGBTQIA+ community as hockey is.

KATE

Achievements

Helen:
- Awarded an <u>MBE</u> in 2017
- Played for Great Britain in the Olympics aged 18
- Has 293 caps for Great Britain

Kate:
- Awarded an <u>OBE</u> in 2014
- Captained Great Britain's women's hockey team for 13 years
- Has over 350 caps for Great Britain

TEAM GB

PARINYA CHAROENPHOL

Born: 1981

Fighting for Change

Parinya Charoenphol grew up in Thailand. At the age of 12, she entered a kickboxing competition and won. She then went on to train in Muay Thai and went on to win many regional fights, making her famous around the country.

Life After Transitioning

Parinya was assigned male at birth and during her kickboxing career she fought as a male. As a teenager, Parinya began to transition from male to female. Eventually she had surgery and stopped boxing professionally. Parinya no longer takes part in professional fights because in many places in Thailand women are not allowed to fight. She now works as a model, actress and performs in boxing shows.

SLAM!

POW!

Achievements

- Won 20 out of 22 regional matches in Muay Thai

- Had the film *Beautiful Boxer* made about her life

- Performs in a one-woman boxing show

I don't think about gender. I think about winning.

BOOM!

MORAN SAMUEL

Born: 1982

A New Challenge

Moran Samuel is an Israeli athlete who began her sporting career playing basketball for Israel's national basketball team. When Moran had a **stroke** that left her **paralysed** from the chest down, she didn't stop practising sports. With the support of her now wife, she began playing wheelchair basketball and practising rowing.

On the Podium

After lots of training, Moran began competing in Paralympic rowing events. She has taken part in many World Championships and World Cups as well as the Paralympic Games. She has won many medals including a bronze at the 2016 Paralympic Games.

Achievements

- Won the Rowing World Championships in 2015
- Came fifth in her first Paralympic Games
- Won gold at the 2015 World Cup

Even the most amazing story in the world will not help you to overcome difficulties in life if you don't realise the strength lies in you.

Creating Waves

Being both a lesbian and a disabled athlete, Moran represents lots of different communities. She is a role model for disabled members of the LGBTQIA+ community. She also <u>campaigns</u> for disabled people and teaches disabled children that they are more than just their <u>impairments</u>.

What Is Representation?

Representation is when lots of different types of people are shown in public. This might be in the <u>media</u>, in sports, or even in schools and communities. Lots of different ages, <u>cultures</u>, sexes and abilities should be represented.

NICOLA ADAMS

Born: 1983

> It's nice to be able to inspire the next generation and for them to have someone to look up to.

> I still achieved and performed at the highest level and I came away with gold and made history so with that said, anything is possible.

TEAM GB

TEAM GB

Entering the Ring

Nicola was born in the north of England. She started boxing at a young age and had her first organised fight at the age of just 13. She started boxing professionally and began winning more and more tournaments. Women's boxing became an Olympic sport in 2012, and Nicola was the first woman to win an Olympic gold medal in the sport. She defended this title at the 2016 Olympics.

Achievements

- First female boxer ever to win an Olympic gold medal

- Awarded an OBE in 2016

- Has won more medals than any other female British boxer

- Named most _influential_ LGBTQIA+ person in Britain in 2012

Punching Down Barriers

Nicola Adams has broken down many barriers in her lifetime. As well as being a role model who has inspired many women to take up boxing, she has also represented and been a role model for the LGBTQIA+ community. She has been labelled by others as bisexual, however Nicola prefers not to label herself as any one particular thing.

LAUREN LUBIN

Born: 1985

> People like myself need to see their own self for once. They need to hear their own story being heard.

Running for Change

Lauren Lubin is a documentary maker and athlete. They are non-binary and choose to use the pronouns they/them. They began playing women's basketball in university, but they soon quit because they were struggling with their gender identity. Over ten years later, Lauren started running. They realised that there weren't many places in sports for non-binary people to be open about their gender. They decided to be the first openly non-binary person to run the New York Marathon to raise awareness of what needs to be done for non-binary people in sports.

My gender is SHUT UP

Achievements

- First non-binary person to run the New York Marathon
- Founder of the non-binary running campaign 'WE RUN'
- Creator of the documentary *We Exist: Beyond the Binary*

Creating Non-Binary Spaces

Lauren has also created spaces for non-binary people by starting a running group in New York that is specifically for non-binary people. They have also created a documentary about their life and the challenges that non-binary people face. Lauren has started conversations about the experiences of non-binary people to try and raise awareness and make changes to their lives.

What's a Pronoun? He/She/They/Them

A person might choose to express their gender identity through the pronouns they use. A non-binary person might use they or them instead of he or she. This might be because they find it hard to identify with either he or she, or they don't agree that gender can be only male or female.

KYE ALLUMS

Born: 1989

> Champions respect other people. We don't have to put other people down... we're all equal.

A Slam Dunk

Kye Allums started playing basketball from a young age and went on to play for the women's team in his university. Kye was assigned female at birth, but for a long time he knew he identified as male. While studying at university he came out to his teammates and coach.

In the Spotlight

Kye became the first openly transgender man to play on a Division 1 basketball team. Kye received a lot of support for coming out to the public and is now an activist who is raising awareness for transgender people in sport.

GEORGE
50
WASHING

50

SLAM DUNK

GEORGE
50
WASHINGTON

50

Achievements

- First openly transgender man to play on a Division 1 basketball team

- Founder of the *I Am Enough* project

What Is Coming Out?

Coming out is when a person chooses to tell someone about their sex, sexuality or gender identity. It is important to remember that a person doesn't have to come out unless they want to or are ready to. A person also doesn't have to come out to everyone they know at once – they can come out to whoever they want, whenever they want. The choice is theirs.

CASTER SEMENYA

Born: 1991

Running for Gold

Caster Semenya first started playing football, but soon began training in athletics. She quickly started beating records for the 800-metre run in South Africa. At the age of 18, she won gold in the 800 metres at the Athletics World Championships.

Undergoing Testing

Semenya ran so fast that many people asked for her to take tests to see what level of testosterone she had. Being a woman with higher levels of testosterone is an intersex condition. The IAAF said that if she wished to compete again, she would have to take medication to lower her levels of testosterone. Semenya refused to do this. She now fights for the rights of female athletes.

Achievements

- Nominated for World Athlete of the Year in 2016
- Has won two Olympic gold medals

What Are the Intersex Rules in Athletics?

Some people think that if a woman has a higher level of testosterone than most women, they might be more likely to win, and this would be unfair to other athletes. The IAAF asks these women to take medication to lower their testosterone levels to make this supposedly fairer.

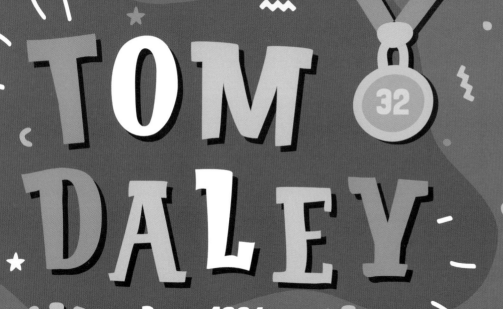

TOM DALEY

32

Born: 1994

> I don't care what people think. I'll do my own thing. I can still dive, I can still do what I want to do.

Making a Splash

Tom Daley began his sporting journey as a swimmer but was quickly seen to have potential in diving. From a very young age he showed a lot of diving talent and by the age of 14, Tom was competing in the Olympic Games. At this young age, Tom was seen as an inspiration for many young people getting into sports.

Telling the World

In 2013, Tom decided to post a video on the internet talking about his sexuality. In the video, he announced that he was in a relationship with a man. They are now married and have started a family. Tom hopes that by being open about his sexuality and family life, it will normalise LGBTQIA+ relationships.

Achievements

- Has won 32 gold medals
- Olympic bronze medallist
- One of the youngest people to ever compete for Great Britain in the Olympics

In an ideal world I wouldn't be doing this video because it shouldn't matter.

BE AN ALLY!

You don't have to be a member of the LGBTQIA+ community to support its members and make sure they are treated equally. Supporting the LGBTQIA+ community is called being an ally. Here are some things you can do to be a good ally in sports.

Include Everyone

If you are playing a game, make sure everyone is included and gets a turn. If you notice someone is being left out on purpose, make sure you ask if they want a turn. If someone is being picked on and doesn't want to play, make sure you tell a grown-up you trust.

Make Space for People

As well as having changing rooms or toilets for just men and women or girls and boys, make sure there is a space for non-binary people as well.

Don't Gender Sports

Instead of having a 'girls team' and a 'boys team', or a 'girls kit' and a 'boys kit', why not just have teams where everyone plays together and the kits are the same for everyone.

PHOTO FINISH

Let's take a look at a few other sportspeople in the LGBTQIA+ community.

Gus Kenworthy
Gus Kenworthy was one of the first openly gay athletes at the Winter Olympics.

Maria José Martínez-Patiño
Maria José Martínez-Patiño was an athlete who was found to be intersex and was banned from women's athletics. She fought this and was able to try out for the 1992 Olympics.

Nadine Angerer
Nadine Angerer is a footballer and is openly bisexual.

Lee Pearson
Lee Pearson is an openly gay Paralympian in **dressage**.

GLOSSARY

abbreviation	a shortened way of writing something
activists	people who try to make a change in the world by doing things such as going to marches
announced	to have told something to a large group of people
assigned	to be given without having a choice
attracted	to want to form a close, romantic or sexual relationship with someone
awareness	to know of or about something
biological sex	whether a person's sex characteristics are considered to be male, female or intersex
biology	the science that studies the growth and life processes of living things
campaigns	takes part in organised ways to reach a goal
caps	in sports, the number of times a person has played for their country's team
chromosomes	tiny things inside cells (the building blocks that make up all living things) that give our bodies information about what to do and how to grow
cisgender	when a person's gender identity matches the biological sex they were assigned at birth
community	a group of people who are connected by something
cranium	the part of the bone in the head that protects the brain
cultures	the traditions, ideas and ways of life of different groups of people
documentary	a film that looks at real facts and events
dressage	a sport that includes training a horse to perform special movements which are controlled by a rider
feminine	things that are stereotypically associated with being female
gender fluid	when a person's gender can switch between male or female or be a mixture of both
genitals	parts of the body between the legs

heterosexual	only being attracted to people of the opposite sex to you
IAAF	International Association of Athletics Federations; the governing body for the sports of athletics across the world
impairments	things that stop or hold a person back from doing something
influential	to have an effect on the behaviour of someone or something, usually in a positive way
march	a large gathering of people who walk from one point to another in order to try to change or celebrate something
masculine	things that are stereotypically associated with being male
MBE	Member of the British Empire, an award given for an outstanding achievement or service to the community
media	the different ways that information is shown to the public such as TV, adverts, newspapers and radio
military	to do with the army
non-binary	a person whose gender identity is not only male or female; non-binary can include people who have no gender, switch between genders or don't identify completely with any one gender
normalise	to make something accepted and normal
OBE	Officer of the Most Excellent Order of the British Empire, an award given to people who have made a great change in their community
organised	when a team of professionals have set up an event
pansexual	when a person can be attracted to anyone regardless of their biological sex, sexuality, gender or gender identity
paralysed	to have lost the ability to move part of the body
professional	doing something you are good at as work
regional	in sports, competitions or games that are played in a certain area
sex characteristics	behaviours or physical features that tell you of a person's biological sex
stereotypes	beliefs which are not founded in facts but are believed by a lot of people
stroke	a serious illness that happens when blood can't get to part of the brain
testosterone	a type of chemical found in both males and females that can affect the muscles and fat in the body

INDEX